Englisch-Stars 4

Erarbeitet von

Barbara Gleich
Irene Reindl
Katrin Schmidt
Britta Schöpe

Illustriert von

Martina Mair und
Wilfried Poll

Cornelsen

Inhalt

Read the comic.

Back to school

1. Fill in the correct sign (< , >).

twenty	◯	twelve
fifteen	◯	thirteen
fourteen	◯	nineteen
eleven	◯	sixteen
eighteen	◯	twenty
seventeen	◯	fifteen

2. Find the words. Write.

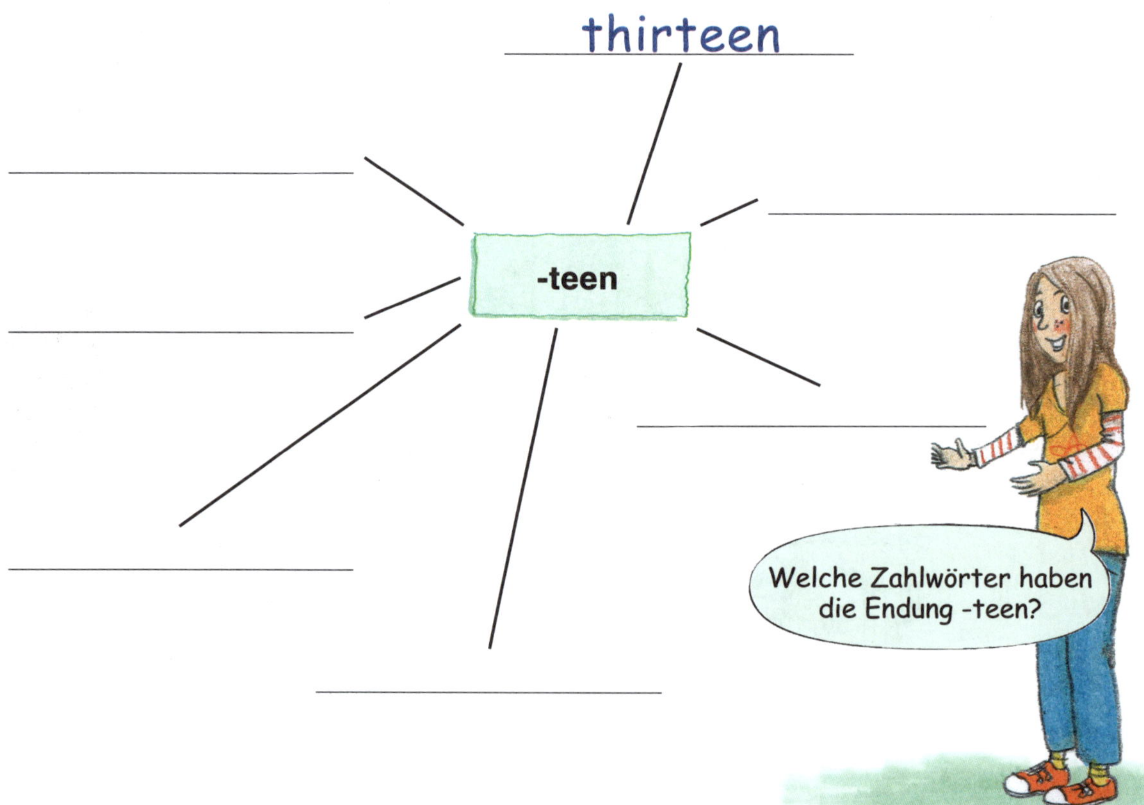

3. How much is it? Fill in.

In Großbritannien bezahlt man mit pounds = £

The helicopter is thirty pounds.

The teddy bear is ________________ pounds.

The computer game is ________________ pounds.

The inline skates are ________________ pounds.

The dress is ________________ pounds.

The boots are ________________ pounds.

The T-shirt is ________________ pounds.

The shoes are ________________ pounds.

The jeans are ________________ pounds.

twenty	**thirty**	**forty**	**fifty**	**sixty**
seventy	**eighty**	**ninety**	**one hundred**	

1. Find the words and circle them. Fill in.

Suche die Wörter senkrecht und waagrecht. Kreise ein. Trage dann unten die durcheinandergeratenen Wörter richtig ein.

k	o	b	a	t	h	r	o	o	m
z	g	c	d	o	o	r	z	k	l
g	a	u	h	i	y	t	i	w	r
f	r	e	a	l	b	g	y	w	b
n	d	h	r	e	v	w	e	i	e
a	e	k	i	t	c	h	e	n	d
z	n	d	e	s	h	f	x	d	r
h	k	g	a	r	a	g	e	o	o
j	s	t	a	i	r	s	b	w	o
l	i	v	i	n	g	r	o	o	m

living room	**toilet**
bedroom	**stairs**
kitchen	**bathroom**
garden	**window**
garage	**door**

Lucy is cooking in the **ikcehtn** ____________ .

Mum is watching TV in the **vngiil mroo** ____________ .

The car is in the **ggraae** ____________ .

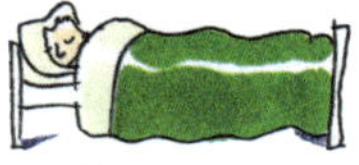

Dad is sleeping in the **dbrmooe** ____________ .

Kevin is playing in the **nraged** ____________ .

Emma is taking a bath in the **ohatobmr** ____________ .

Sally is reading on the **otielt** ____________ .

2. What is it? Complete and draw lines.

Was hat sich hinter den Bildausschnitten versteckt? Vervollständige erst die Wörter und verbinde dann mit dem richtigen Bild.

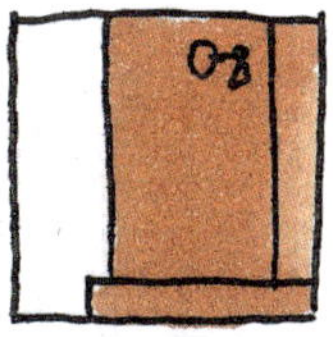

ch _ _ r

_ ab _ _

_ e _

l _ m _

w _ _ dr _ b _

s _ _ _ _ _ _ s

_ es _

s _ f _

lamp
table
bed
sofa
wardrobe
shelves
desk
chair

3. Find the furniture and colour the fields brown. What can you see?

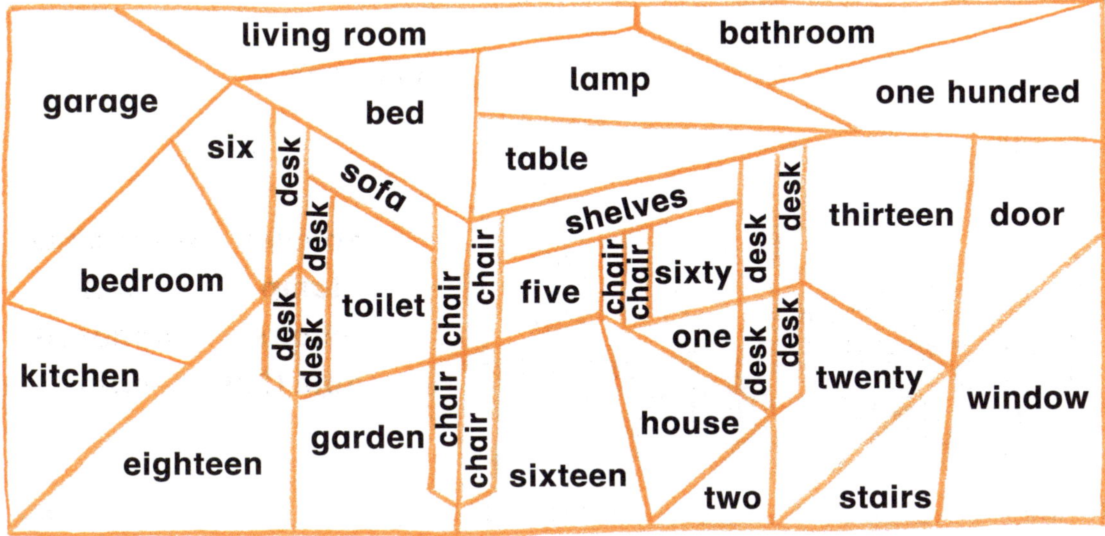

I can see a ______________________________________ .

4. Describe the rooms. Fill in.

Was gibt es alles in den verschiedenen Räumen zu sehen? Schreibe auf.

In the ______________ there's a ______________ and two ______________ .

bedroom
kitchen
living room

In the ______________ there's a ______________ , a ______________ , a ______________ and three ______________ .

shelves	**wardrobes**
lamp	**bed**
chairs	**cupboard**
table (2x)	**sofa**

In the ______________ there's a ______________ with four ______________ and a ______________ .

5. Crazy rooms. Read and number.

Welche Beschreibung passt zu welchem Zimmer?

1

2

3

◯ My room is purple. I've got a table with three chairs and a pink bed. I've also got a pink toilet and a small garden.

◯ My room has got a small bed, a small desk with a chair and two big shelves.

◯ I live in a very dark room. In my room there's a red sofa and a black wardrobe. I don't like lamps.

6. Read the comic.

Is there a room for me?

My home is a big house with three big bedrooms. One for Mum and Dad, one for me and one for you. Come and live with me.

That's great. Thank you.

1. Find the words. Draw lines and write.

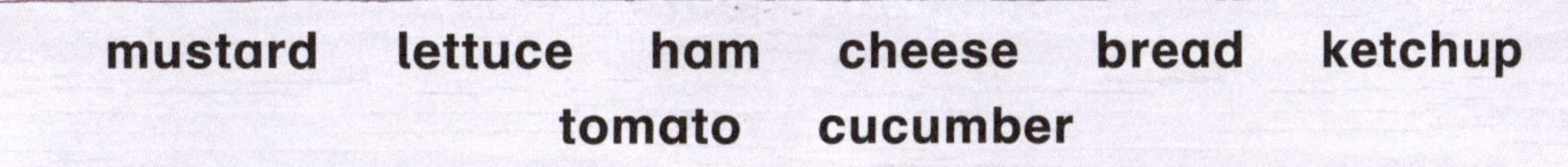

mustard **lettuce** **ham** **cheese** **bread** **ketchup**
tomato **cucumber**

2. Read and draw lines.

3. What is it? Read and write.

It's brown and soft.	It's ______________ .
It's green and long.	It's a ______________ .
It's yellow and a mouse likes it.	It's ______________ .
It's yellow, but it's not cheese.	It's ______________ .
It's green and has got leaves.	It's ______________ .
It's pink and part of an animal.	It's ______________ .
It's red and looks like a small ball.	It's a ______________ .
It's red, but it's not a tomato.	It's ______________ .

bread tomato cheese ham cucumber ketchup mustard lettuce

4. Write and draw lines.

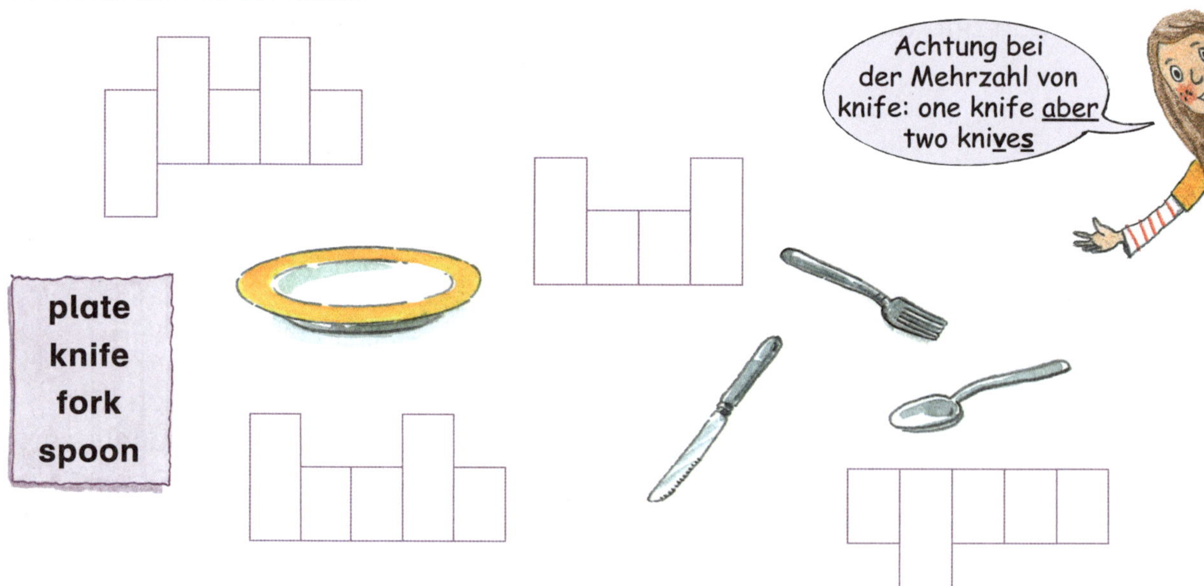

5. What's on the menu? Number and write.

6. Look at the menu again. Do you know what the children want? Write.

Die bestellen ja alles völlig verdreht! Schreibe es richtig auf.

I'd like spaghetti soup and a carrot.

____.

I'd like a fish salad and chicken and chips.

____.

I'd like a mashed carrot and a sausage soup with potatoes.

____

____.

7. Complete the dialogue. Write.

pizza drink eat Here you are Thank you
coke lemonade sausage with mashed potatoes

8. Read the comic.

Sally likes lollipops

Zeichne die Uhrzeiger richtig ein und spure dann die Sätze nach.

1. Draw the clock's hands and write.

It's two o'clock.

It's six o'clock.

It's eleven o'clock.

2. What time is it? Write.

nine	eight
five	three
twelve	

It's three o'clock .

______________________________ .

______________________________ .

______________________________ .

______________________________ .

3. Write and draw lines.

Lucy's day

get up	**play with my friends**
do my homework	**have breakfast**
go to bed and sleep	**go to school**

I have breakfast ______________________

I ______________________

____

in the morning.

I ______________________

____

in the afternoon.

I ______________________

____

in the evening /

at night.

I ______________________

____

I ______________________

____

4. An interview. Read and fill in.

Hello, Ben.	Hello, ________ (your name).
When do you get up?	I get up at ________ o'clock.
When do you start school?	I start ________ ________.
When do you do your homework?	I do my ________ ________.
When do you play with your friends?	I play with my ________ ________.
When do you go to bed and sleep?	I go ________ ________.
Thank you for the interview. Goodbye.	You're welcome. Bye.

5. Read the comic.

Time for breakfast?

1. Trace the lines and write.

_______________ likes riding a mountain bike.

_______________ likes reading books.

_______________ likes swimming.

_______________ likes riding a horse.

_______________ likes playing football.

_______________ likes snowboarding.

_______________ likes playing the piano.

_______________ likes ice skating.

_______________ likes playing the guitar.

2. Guess the hobby. Read and write.

Linda's hobby is ____________________ .

Ron's ____________________ .

Betty's ____________________ .

Sam's ____________________ .

Kathy's ____________________

____________________ .

David's ____________________

____________________ .

snowboarding	**reading books**	**riding a horse**
swimming	**playing the piano**	**playing football**

3. Look at the pictures and write.

Can Jane play tennis? Yes, she can.

Can Harry play football? No, he can't.

Can Jane ice skate? ____________________

Can Bill ride a horse? ____________________

Can Harry play tennis? ____________________

Can Jane play the guitar? ____________________

Can Bill play basketball? ____________________

Can Harry swim? ____________________

Can Bill ride a skateboard? ____________________

Denke daran: Verwende bei Jungen **he**, bei Mädchen **she**.

And what can you do?

I can ____________________

____

4. Read and fill in.

Hello. What's your name?

Hi. My ______________ is Tom.

______________ your name?

____________________ is Helen.

What's your favourite hobby?

My favourite ______________ is ________________________

______________ ⚽ .

What's your ____ ?

I like ______________________________________ ⚽ , too.

Let's play together!

Good idea! Let's go!

1. At the shopping centre. Write.

In the supermarket I can buy ______________________ .

In the music shop I ______________________ .

______________________ .

______________________ .

______________________ .

______________________ .

______________________ .

______________________ .

orange juice **CDs** **books** **shoes** **lollipops**
pullovers **inline skates** **teddy bears**

2. In the clothes shop. Write.

Are the clothes just right?

No, the jacket is too big.

Yes, the dress is just right.

______________________________.

______________________________.

______________________________.

too big	too small	just right	pullover	dress
shoes	skirt	jacket		

Wem gehört welcher Einkaufskorb? Ergänze die fehlenden Dinge.

3. In the supermarket. Whose shopping basket is it? Add the missing things to the list.

Sarah
coffee, eggs, ______________

____

____

George
bananas, milk, ______________

____

____

Andy
pineapple, ham, ______________

____

____

Olivia
bread, coke, ______________

____

____

butter	**honey**	**lemonade**	**bacon**	**cherries**	**tea**	**spinach**
jam	**milk**	**oranges**	**water**	**chocolate bars**	**eggs**	**rolls**
cheese	**apple juice**	**cornflakes**	**biscuits**			

4. In the sports shop. Read and number.

 It's £30.

Here you are. Goodbye.

 Thank you. Bye.

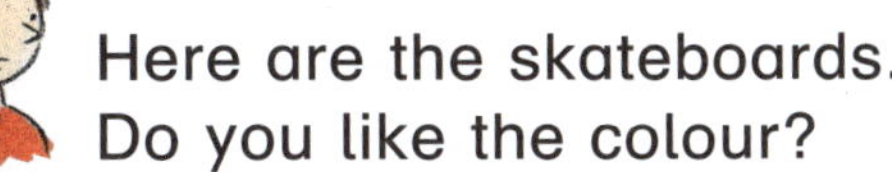 Here are the skateboards. Do you like the colour?

 No, sorry. I don't like red.

 Hello. Can I help you?

Hello. I'd like a new skateboard.

 Do you like the green skateboard?

 It's perfect. Green is my favourite colour!

5. Read the comic.

Sally goes shopping

1. Find the correct word. Write.

1=a	6=f	11=l	16=s
2=b	7=g	12=n	17=t
3=c	8=h	13=o	18=u
4=d	9=i	14=p	19=x
5=e	10=k	15=r	20=y

_ _ _
3 1 15

_ _ _ _
2 9 10 5

_ _ _ _ _
14 11 1 12 5

_ _ _ _
17 1 19 9

_ _ _ _ _ _ _ _ _ _ _
18 12 4 5 15 7 15 13 18 12 4

_ _ _ _ _
11 13 15 15 20

_ _ _ _
2 13 1 17

_ _ _ _ _ _ _ _ _ _
8 5 11 9 3 13 14 17 5 15

_ _ _ _ _
17 15 1 9 12

_ _ _
2 18 16

2. Sally likes to travel. Write.

train	boat	car	plane

 I go to London by ______________________.

 I go to Scotland by ______________________.

 I go to see my friend ______________________.

 I go to see the Queen ______________________.

3. Trace the lines and write.

Bob is going by ______________________.

Sandy is ______________________.

Tim ______________________.

Ann ______________________.

4. Number the traffic signs.

1 **straight on**

2 **turn left**

3 **turn right**

5. Where are the children going? Find the ways.

Tom: Turn left, go straight on, turn left again and then turn right.

Tom is going to the ______________________________________ .

Susan: Go straight on, then turn right, go straight on and then turn right again.

Susan is ______________________________________ .

Kim: Turn right, go straight on, turn left, then go straight on again and turn left again.

Kim ______________________________________ .

Lies erst die Wegbeschreibung und fahre denWeg auf dem Plan nach. Verbinde dann die Frage mit der richtigen Wegbeschreibung.

6. Look at the map. Read and trace the way. Connect the answers and the questions. Fill in the missing words.

How do I get to the cinema, please?	Go straight on.Turn right into Baker Street. Turn left into River Street. The ____________________ is on the right.
How do I get to the book shop, please?	Turn left into Church Street. Turn right into School Street. Turn right again into Main Street. The ______________ is on the left.
How do I get to the computer shop, please?	Turn left into Church Street. Go straight on.Turn right into School Street. Cross Main Street. The __________________ is on the right.

Informationen für Eltern und Lehrkräfte

Englisch spielerisch üben mit den Englisch-Stars

Aufbau und Gestaltung der Englisch-Stars

Mit den Englisch-Stars üben und sichern die Kinder auf spielerische Weise den für die Grundschule wichtigen Wortschatz sowie ihr Lese- und Schreibvermögen. Abwechslungsreiche Übungsformen und ansprechende Illustrationen motivieren, Wörter und Strukturen vielfältig anzuwenden.

Das Känguru Sally ist dabei ständiger Begleiter. Die beiden deutschsprachigen Kinder Lisa und Max unterstützen mit Tipps und Hilfestellungen.

Die Englisch-Stars sind unterteilt in verschiedene Themenbereiche, die unabhängig voneinander bearbeitet werden können. Zusätzlich bieten sie im Anhang ein kleines Picture dictionary (Bildwörterbuch). Zu jedem Thema gibt es dort eine Seite, die den Wortschatz einführt. Daher ist es empfehlenswert, diese jeweils als Erstes zu bearbeiten.
Im Anschluss folgen vielfältige Übungen zur Wortschatzwiederholung und -sicherung sowie zur Sicherung des Lese- und Schreibvermögens, z.B. Zuordnungsaufgaben, Bilderrätsel und Dialoge. Lustige Comics mit Sally zeigen den Kindern, wie viel sie schon selbstständig lesen und verstehen können.
Eindeutige Aufgabenstellungen und Selbstkontrolle durch den Lösungsteil ermöglichen den Kindern, eigenständig mit den Englisch-Stars zu arbeiten.

Für jede Seite im Picture dictionary, nach jedem Thema, für jeden gelesenen Comic und für besonders schwierige Aufgaben (Sternchenaufgaben) dürfen sich die Kinder mit einem Sternchen-Aufkleber belohnen. Als besonderer Anreiz ergeben die Sterne am Ende des Heftes ein Gesamtbild.

Die Englisch-Stars dienen der spielerischen und zwanglosen Auseinandersetzung mit Englisch und fördern die Freude am Erlernen der Fremdsprache.

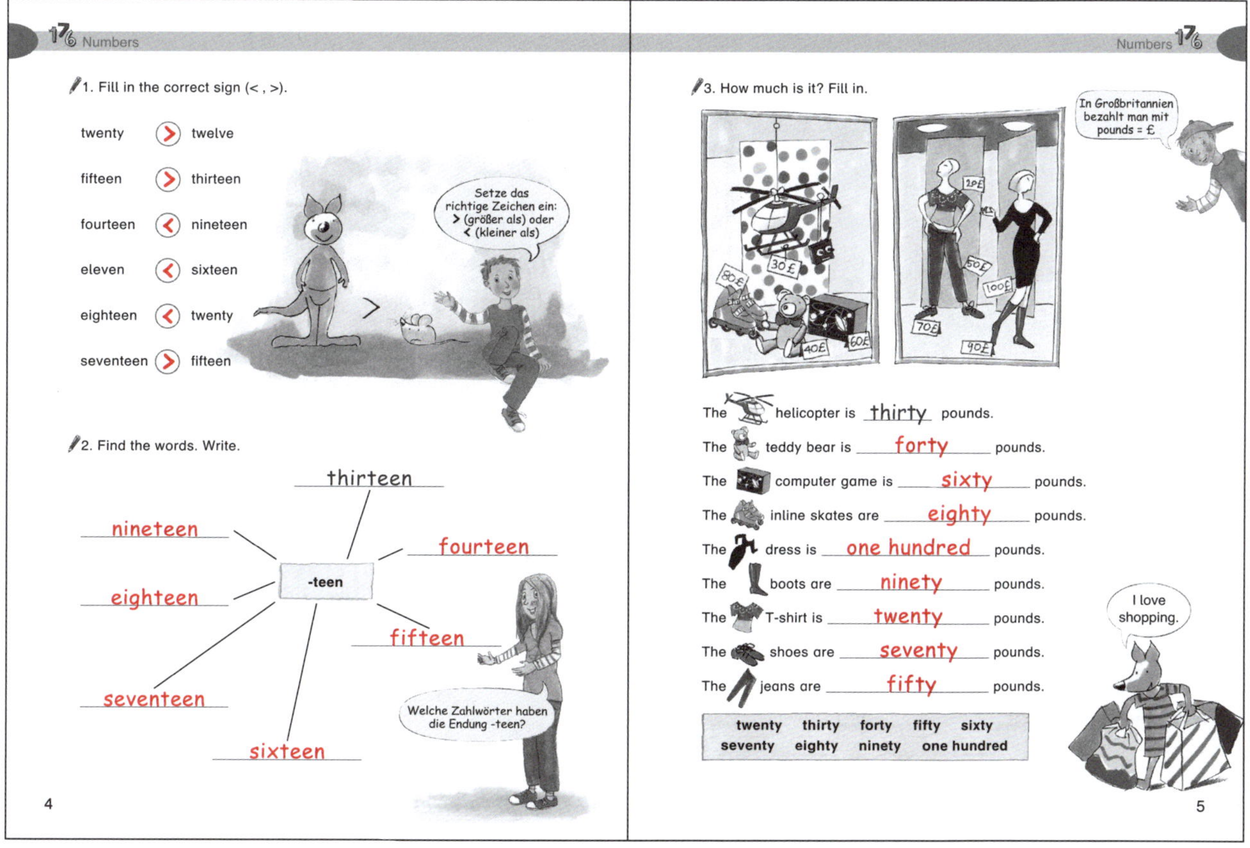

Numbers

1. Fill in the correct sign (< , >).

twenty > twelve
fifteen > thirteen
fourteen < nineteen
eleven < sixteen
eighteen < twenty
seventeen > fifteen

2. Find the words. Write.

-teen: thirteen, fourteen, fifteen, sixteen, seventeen, eighteen, nineteen

4

Numbers

3. How much is it? Fill in.

The helicopter is thirty pounds.
The teddy bear is forty pounds.
The computer game is sixty pounds.
The inline skates are eighty pounds.
The dress is one hundred pounds.
The boots are ninety pounds.
The T-shirt is twenty pounds.
The shoes are seventy pounds.
The jeans are fifty pounds.

twenty thirty forty fifty sixty
seventy eighty ninety one hundred

5

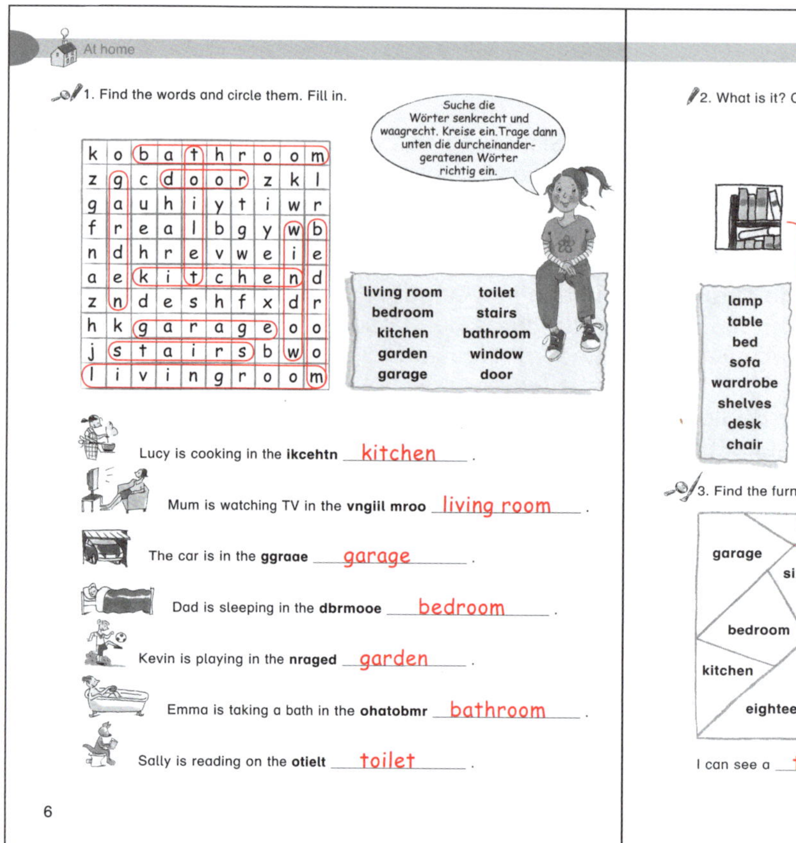

1. Find the words and circle them. Fill in.

k	o	b	a	t	h	r	o	o	m
z	g	c	d	o	o	r	z	k	l
g	a	u	h	i	y	t	i	w	r
f	r	e	a	l	b	g	y	w	b
n	d	h	r	e	v	w	e	i	e
a	e	k	i	t	c	h	e	n	d
z	n	d	e	s	h	f	x	d	r
h	k	g	a	r	a	g	e	o	o
j	s	t	a	i	r	s	b	w	o
l	i	v	i	n	g	r	o	o	m

living room	**toilet**
bedroom	**stairs**
kitchen	**bathroom**
garden	**window**
garage	**door**

Lucy is cooking in the **ikcehtn** kitchen.

Mum is watching TV in the **vngiil mroo** living room.

The car is in the **ggraae** garage.

Dad is sleeping in the **dbrmooe** bedroom.

Kevin is playing in the **nraged** garden.

Emma is taking a bath in the **ohatobmr** bathroom.

Sally is reading on the **otielt** toilet.

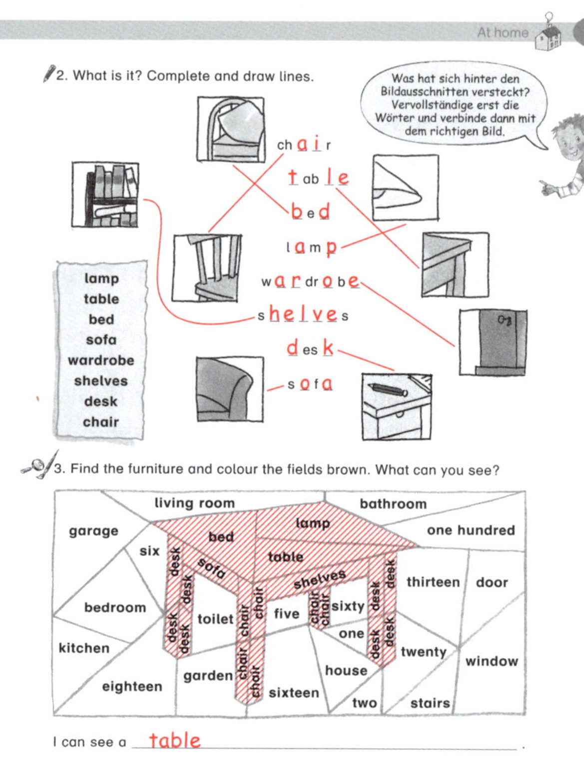

2. What is it? Complete and draw lines.

lamp
table
bed
sofa
wardrobe
shelves
desk
chair

3. Find the furniture and colour the fields brown. What can you see?

I can see a table.

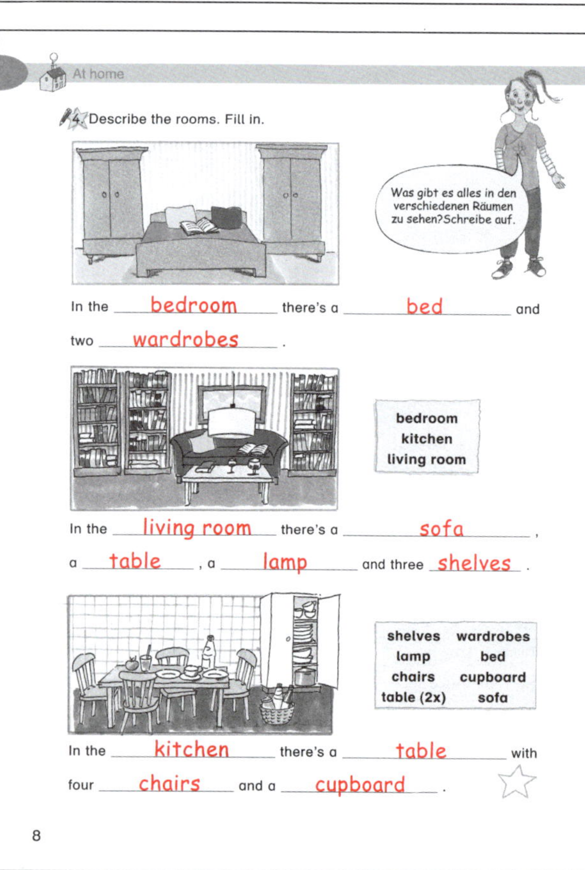

4. Describe the rooms. Fill in.

In the bedroom there's a bed and two wardrobes.

bedroom
kitchen
living room

In the living room there's a sofa, a table, a lamp and three shelves.

shelves	**wardrobes**
lamp	**bed**
chairs	**cupboard**
table (2x)	**sofa**

In the kitchen there's a table with four chairs and a cupboard.

5. Crazy rooms. Read and number.

(3) My room is purple. I've got a table with three chairs and a pink bed. I've also got a pink toilet and a small garden.

(1) My room has got a small bed, a small desk with a chair and two big shelves.

(2) I live in a very dark room. In my room there's a red sofa and a black wardrobe. I don't like lamps.

6. Read the comic.

Is there a room for me?

1. Find the words. Draw lines and write.

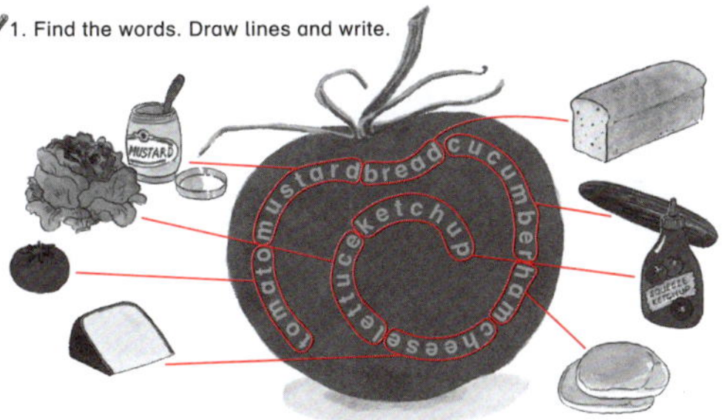

tomato, mustard, bread, cucumber, ham, cheese, lettuce, ketchup

mustard lettuce ham cheese bread ketchup tomato cucumber

2. Read and draw lines.

3. What is it? Read and write.

It's brown and soft.	It's bread.
It's green and long.	It's a cucumber.
It's yellow and a mouse likes it.	It's cheese.
It's yellow, but it's not cheese.	It's mustard.
It's green and has got leaves.	It's lettuce.
It's pink and part of an animal.	It's ham.
It's red and looks like a small ball.	It's a tomato.
It's red, but it's not a tomato.	It's ketchup.

bread tomato cheese ham cucumber ketchup mustard lettuce

4. Write and draw lines.

plate knife fork spoon

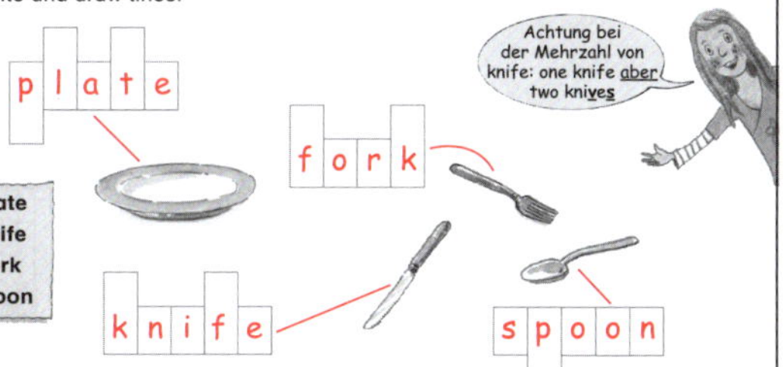

plate

fork

knife

spoon

5. What's on the menu? Number and write.

1. carrot soup	£3.00	4. fish and chips	£5.00
2. pizza	£5.00	5. sausage with mashed potatoes	£7.50
3. spaghetti	£5.50	6. chicken salad	£4.50

6. Look at the menu again. Do you know what the children want? Write.

I'd like spaghetti soup and a carrot.

I'd like spaghetti and a carrot soup.

I'd like a fish salad and chicken and chips.

I'd like a chicken salad and fish and chips.

I'd like a mashed carrot and a sausage soup with potatoes.

I'd like a carrot soup and a sausage with mashed potatoes.

7. Complete the dialogue. Write.

What would you like to **eat**?

We'd like a **sausage with mashed potatoes** and a **pizza**, please.

Would you like something to **drink**, too?

We'd like a **coke** and a **lemonade**, please.

Here you are.

Thank you.

That's twenty pounds.

Here you are

pizza drink eat Here you are Thank you
coke lemonade sausage with mashed potatoes

8. Read the comic.

Sally likes lollipops

1. Draw the clock's hands and write.

It's two o'clock.

It's six o'clock.

It's eleven o'clock.

2. What time is it? Write.

nine eight
five three
twelve

It's three o'clock.

It's eight o'clock.

It's twelve o'clock.

It's five o'clock.

It's nine o'clock.

3. Write and draw lines.

Lucy's day

get up play with my friends
do my homework have breakfast
go to bed and sleep go to school

I have breakfast — in the morning.

I **do my homework** — in the afternoon.

I **get up** — in the morning.

I **play with my friends** — in the afternoon.

I **go to bed and sleep** — in the evening / at night.

I **go to school** — in the morning.

4. An interview. Read and fill in.

Hello, Ben. — Hello, ___ (your name).

When do you get up? — I get up at seven o'clock.

When do you start school? — I start school at nine o'clock.

When do you do your homework? — I do my homework at four o'clock.

When do you play with your friends? — I play with my friends at five o'clock.

When do you go to bed and sleep? — I go to bed and sleep at nine o'clock.

Thank you for the interview. Goodbye. — You're welcome. Bye.

5. Read the comic.

Time for breakfast?

1. Trace the lines and write.

Eric likes **riding a mountain bike**.

John likes **reading books**.

Kim likes **swimming**.

Judy likes **riding a horse**.

Nick likes **playing football**.

Andy likes **snowboarding**.

Lucy likes **playing the piano**.

Emma likes **ice skating**.

Martha likes **playing the guitar**.

2. Guess the hobby. Read and write.

Linda's hobby is snowboarding.

Ron's hobby is riding a horse.

Betty's hobby is swimming.

Sam's hobby is playing the piano.

Kathy's hobby is playing football.

David's hobby is reading books.

snowboarding **reading books** **riding a horse** **swimming** **playing the piano** **playing football**

3. Look at the pictures and write.

Jane Harry Bill

Can Jane play tennis?	Yes, she can.
Can Harry play football?	No, he can't.
Can Jane ice skate?	No, she can't.
Can Bill ride a horse?	Yes, he can.
Can Harry play tennis?	No, he can't.
Can Jane play the guitar?	Yes, she can.
Can Bill play basketball?	No, he can't.
Can Harry swim?	Yes, he can.
Can Bill ride a skateboard?	Yes, he can.

Denke daran: Verwende bei Jungen **he**, bei Mädchen **she**.

And what can you do?

I can ______

4. Read and fill in.

Hello. What's your name?

Hi. My name is Tom.
What's your name?

My name is Helen.
What's your favourite hobby?

My favourite hobby is playing football.
What's your favourite hobby?

I like playing football, too.
Let's play together!

Good idea! Let's go!

And I like playing football, too.

1. At the shopping centre. Write.

SUPERMARKET MUSIC SHOP CLOTHES SHOP SWEET SHOP TOY SHOP BOOK SHOP SPORTS SHOP SHOE SHOP

In the supermarket I can buy orange juice.
In the music shop I can buy CDs.
In the clothes shop I can buy pullovers.
In the sweet shop I can buy lollipops.
In the toy shop I can buy teddy bears.
In the book shop I can buy books.
In the sports shop I can buy inline skates.
In the shoe shop I can buy shoes.

orange juice CDs books shoes lollipops pullovers inline skates teddy bears

2. In the clothes shop. Write.

Are the clothes just right?

No, the jacket is too big.

Yes, the dress is just right.

No, the pullover is too small.

No, the shoes are too big.

Yes, the skirt is just right.

too big too small just right pullover dress shoes skirt jacket

Wem gehört welcher Einkaufskorb? Ergänze die fehlenden Dinge.

3. In the supermarket. Whose shopping basket is it? Add the missing things to the list.

George

Andy

Olivia

Sarah

Sarah
coffee, eggs, cherries, lemonade, spinach, jam

George
bananas, milk, honey, biscuits, water, apple juice

Andy
pineapple, ham, butter, cornflakes, milk, cheese, tea, rolls

Olivia
bread, coke, oranges, chocolate bars, eggs, bacon

butter	honey	lemonade	bacon	cherries	tea	spinach
jam	milk	oranges	water	chocolate bars	eggs	rolls
cheese	apple juice	cornflakes	biscuits			

4. In the sports shop. Read and number.

1 2 3 4

④
It's £30.
Here you are. Goodbye.
Thank you. Bye.

①
Hello. Can I help you?
Hello. I'd like a new skateboard.

②
Here are the skateboards. Do you like the colour?
No, sorry. I don't like red.

③
Do you like the green skateboard?
It's perfect. Green is my favourite colour!

5. Read the comic.

Sally goes shopping

Sally, can you please go to the supermarket for me? Here is the shopping list.
spinach eggs potatoes bread butter cheese
Okay Mum. Bye.
I don't like spinach and potatoes.
bread
eggs
cheese
potatoes
butter
spinach
But I like chocolate, apples, strawberries and lemonade.
Oh no, Sally. And what do we eat for dinner now?
Oh Mum! This dinner is fantastic.

1. Find the correct word. Write.

car
3 1 15

bike
2 9 10 5

plane
14 11 1 12 5

taxi
17 1 19 9

lorry
11 13 15 15 20

helicopter
8 5 11 9 3 13 14 17 5 15

train
17 15 1 9 12

underground
18 12 4 5 15 7 15 13 18 12 4

boat
2 13 1 17

bus
2 18 16

1=a	6=f	11=l	16=s
2=b	7=g	12=n	17=t
3=c	8=h	13=o	18=u
4=d	9=i	14=p	19=x
5=e	10=k	15=r	20=y

Vehicles

2. Sally likes to travel. Write.

train boat car plane

I go to London by plane.

I go to Scotland by train.

I go to see my friend by boat.

I go to see the Queen by car.

3. Trace the lines and write.

Bob is going by car.

Sandy is going by train.

Tim is going by bike.

Ann is going by plane.

30

Vehicles

4. Number the traffic signs.

1 straight on
2 turn left
3 turn right

2 3 1

5. Where are the children going? Find the ways.

Tom: Turn left, go straight on, turn left again and then turn right.

Tom is going to the pet shop.

Susan: Go straight on, then turn right, go straight on and then turn right again.

Susan is going to the supermarket.

Kim: Turn right, go straight on, turn left, then go straight on again and turn left again.

Kim is going to the music shop.

31

Vehicles

6. Look at the map. Read and trace the way. Connect the answers and the questions. Fill in the missing words.

How do I get to the cinema, please? — Go straight on. Turn right into Baker Street. Turn left into River Street. The computer shop is on the right.

How do I get to the book shop, please? — Turn left into Church Street. Turn right into School Street. Turn right again into Main Street. The cinema is on the left.

How do I get to the computer shop, please? — Turn left into Church Street. Go straight on. Turn right into School Street. Cross Main Street. The book shop is on the right.

32

Wild animals

1. At the zoo you can see a lot of wild animals. Do you know them? Write.

elephant lion giraffe monkey hippo zebra crocodile kangaroo

33

2. Match the legs to the animals. Draw lines and write.

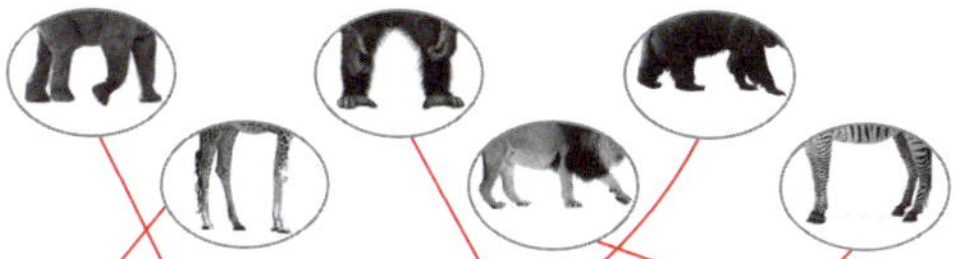

giraffe elephant bear monkey zebra lion

3. What can the animals do? Write the correct answer.

Yes, it can. No, it can't.

Can a crocodile fly? No, it can't.

Can a hippo swim? Yes, it can.

Can a snake jump? No, it can't.

Can a monkey jump? Yes, it can.

Can a bear swim? Yes, it can.

Can a lion fly? No, it can't.

Richtig oder falsch? Schreibe die Antwort auf.

4. Funny animals. Write and draw.

head: giraffe

body: lion

legs: elephant

head: koala

body: snake

legs: kangaroo

head: bear

body: monkey

legs: crocodile

Now draw this animal:

The head is from a kangaroo.

The body is from a hippo.

The legs are from a zebra.

Kopf: Känguru

Körper: Nilpferd

Beine: Zebra

5. Find out their favourite animals. Read and write.

Wir sollen die Lieblingstiere von Tim, Ben, Mary, Jenny und Sally herausfinden.

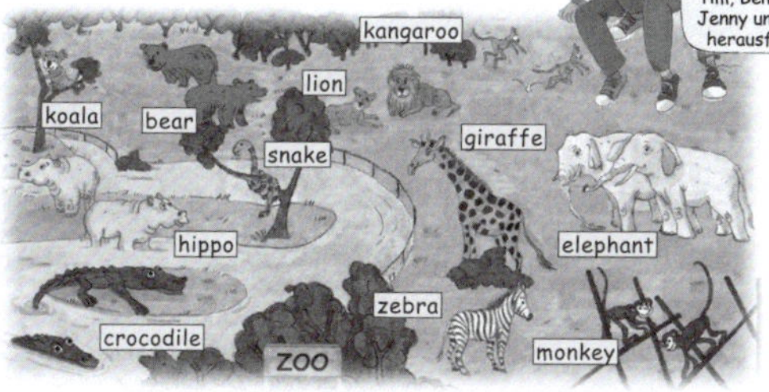

kangaroo, lion, koala, bear, snake, giraffe, hippo, elephant, zebra, crocodile, monkey, ZOO

Tim: My favourite animal is green. It has got a big mouth with sharp teeth. My favourite animal is a crocodile.

Ben: My favourite animal is grey and has got a long nose. My favourite animal is an elephant.

Mary: And my favourite animal is brown and likes bananas. My favourite animal is a monkey.

Jenny: My animal is brown and yellow and has got a long neck. My favourite animal is a giraffe.

Sally: My favourite animal is brown and can jump. My favourite animal is a kangaroo.

6. Read the comic.

Sally and Koala at the zoo

Lösungen

1. Fill in.

-ache: back, ear, stomach, tooth, head

head	back
ear	tooth
stomach	

2. Fill in and draw lines.

Sally's ear hurts. She has got an earache.

Sally's tooth hurts. She has got a toothache.

Sally's back hurts. She has got a backache.

Sally's head hurts. She has got a headache.

Sally's stomach hurts. She has got a stomachache.

headache earache stomachache backache toothache

3. What's the matter? Read and fill in.

I have eaten 5 pizzas. — You have got a stomachache.

I have fallen from a tree. — You have got a broken arm.

My nose is running. — You have got a cold.

My head feels hot. — You have got a fever.

I have carried ten boxes of lollipops. — You have got a backache.

cold broken arm backache fever stomachache

4. Read and fill in.

Ben is sitting in the waiting room.

The nurse comes in and says: "Next, please!"

It's Ben's turn. The doctor asks Ben: "What's the matter?"

"I'm ill. I've got a headache, I've got a fever and I think I've got a cold, too. I can't go to school today."

The doctor says: "Ben, you are not ill. Why can't you go to school today?"

"We have got a math test today, Daddy."

doctor (2x) fever nurse headache cold waiting room

5. Read the comic.

A lollipop will help

1. Guess the jobs. Write.

Sally is a hairdresser.

Sally is a doctor.

Sally is a teacher.

Sally is a policewoman and Koala is a policeman.

Sally is a shop assistant.

Sally is an actress and Koala is an actor.

Koala is a vet.

Sally is a football player.

shop assistant
hairdresser
teacher
doctor
policewoman/ policeman
actress/ actor
vet
football player

2. My jobs at home. Draw lines and write.

make	the cat
feed	my bed
help	my room
do	in the kitchen
walk	in the garden
tidy	the dog
help	my homework

I have to make my bed.

I have to feed the cat.

I have to help in the garden.

I have to do my homework.

I have to walk the dog.

I have to tidy my room.

I have to help in the kitchen.

3. Look at Sandy, Jack and Sally.
Which jobs do they like and which not? Write.

I like to help in the kitchen, but
I don't like to make my bed.

I like to do my homework, but
I don't like to clean my room.

I like to feed the cat,
but I don't like to help in the garden.

And what about you? Write.

I ____________________,

but ____________________.

4. Read the comic.

Sally, what do you want to be?

Lösungen

1. Where are the children from? Write.

Grmeany — I'm from Germany.

SUA — I'm from the USA .

Sipan — I'm from Spain .

Garte Bnariti — I'm from Great Britain .

Fneacr — I'm from France .

Pnoald — I'm from Poland .

Terkyu — I'm from Turkey .

Rsasiu — I'm from Russia .

Iaytl — I'm from Italy .

Turkey Italy USA Russia France Great Britain Spain Germany Poland

2. Guess the country. Read and write.

I love to eat baguette and croissants. I say "Bonjour!" and not "Hello!". The capital of my country is Paris.
I'm from France .

The name of our flag is Union Jack. The capital of my country is London. We have a Queen.
I'm from Great Britain .

I eat spaghetti almost every day. But I also like to eat pizza. The capital of my country is Rome.
I'm from Italy .

The capital of my country is Berlin. I say "Hallo!".
I'm from Germany .

I don't say "Hello!", I say "Merhaba!". A lot of people come to my country for their holidays. The capital of my country is Ankara.
I'm from Turkey .

Turkey France Germany Italy Great Britain

3. Read and fill in.

Are you from Germany ?
Yes, I am. Are you from Germany , too?
No, I'm not. I'm from Italy .

Are you from the USA ?
No, I'm not . I'm from Spain .

Hello, I'm from Great Britain . Are you from Great Britain , too?
No, I'm not . I'm from Russia .

Are you from Turkey ?
Yes, I am . Are you from Spain ?
No, I'm not . I'm from Poland .

USA Spain Poland Russia Germany Turkey Great Britain Italy

4. Read the comic.

Sally's trip around the world

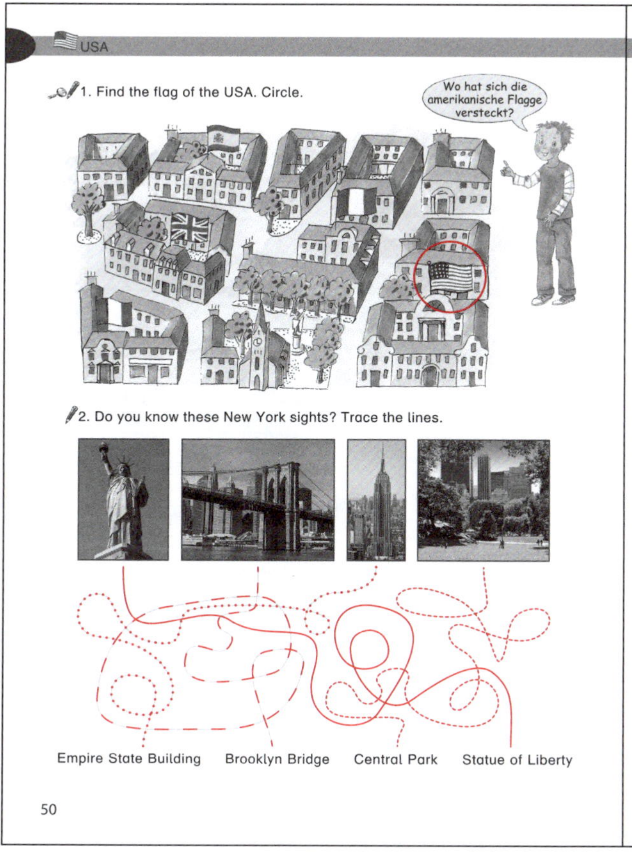

USA

1. Find the flag of the USA. Circle.

2. Do you know these New York sights? Trace the lines.

50

USA

3. Where's Sally? Draw lines and write.

51

USA

4. Circle the correct name of the USA.

the United Stars of America

the United States of America

the United Stripes of America

5. Correct or wrong? Tick.

	correct	wrong
The name of the flag of the USA is Union Jack.		X
Americans pay with dollars and cents.	X	
New York is one of the biggest cities in the USA.	X	
The Empire State Building is a small house.		X
Central Park is a big park in New York.	X	
The Queen is the president of the USA.		X
The people in the USA speak English.	X	
The capital of the USA is London.		X
The capital of the USA is Washington D.C.	X	

52

Picture dictionary: Numbers

eleven twelve thirteen fourteen fifteen sixteen seventeen eighteen nineteen twenty thirty forty fifty sixty seventy eighty ninety one hundred

53

In the morning:

I get up at seven o'clock.

I have breakfast at eight o'clock.

School starts at nine o'clock.

In the afternoon:

I do my homework at three o'clock.

What time is it?

It's four o'clock.

I play with my friends at four o'clock.

In the evening / at night:

I go to bed and sleep at nine o'clock.

riding a mountain bike

skateboarding

reading books

swimming

playing tennis

ice skating

snowboarding

playing football

playing basketball

playing the guitar

riding a horse

inline skating

playing the piano

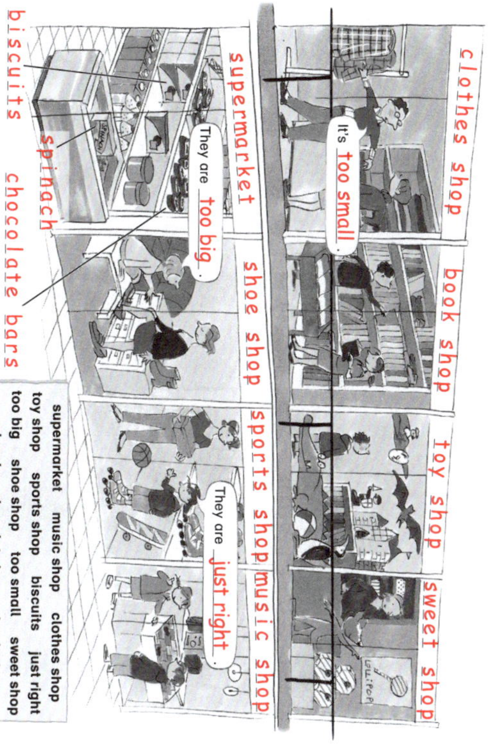

biscuits
spinach
chocolate bars
supermarket
They are too big.
shoe shop
sports shop
music shop
They are just right.
clothes shop
It's too small.
book shop
toy shop
sweet shop

supermarket music shop clothes shop
toy shop sports shop biscuits just right
too big shoe shop too small sweet shop
spinach chocolate bars book shop

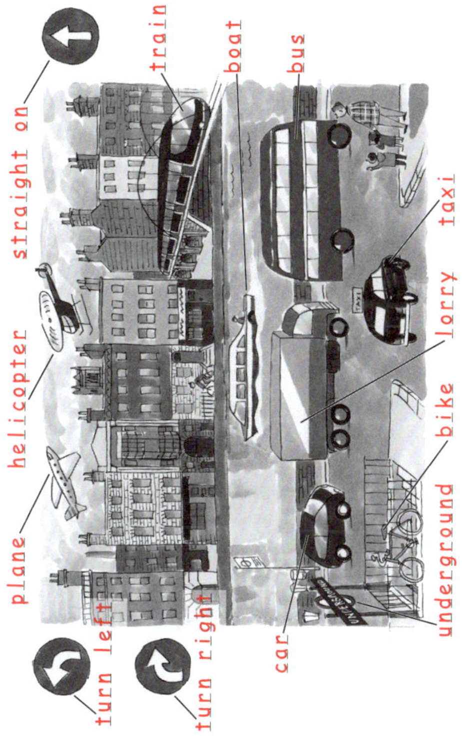

straight on
train
boat
bus
helicopter
taxi
lorry
bike
plane
underground
car
turn left
turn right

bus taxi bike car underground train lorry plane helicopter boat
straight on turn right turn left

koala zebra lion snake hippo giraffe elephant
monkey crocodile kangaroo bear

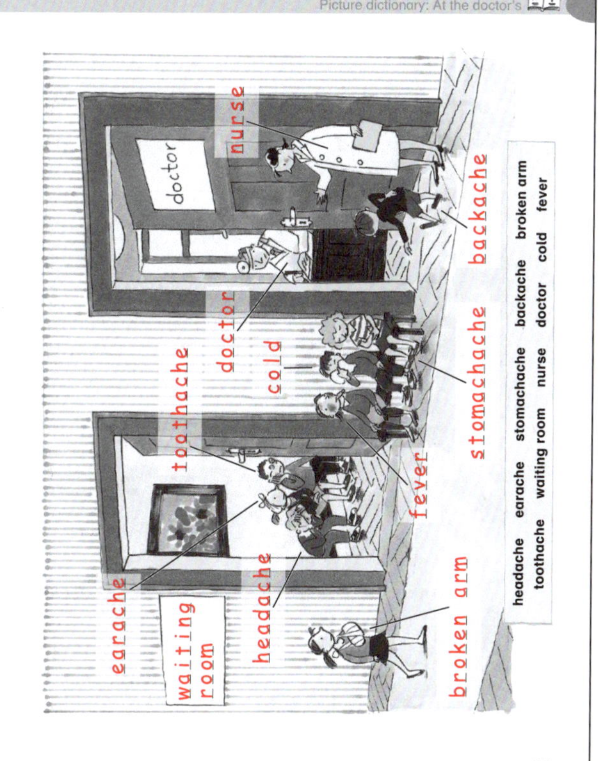

headache earache stomachache backache broken arm
toothache waiting room nurse doctor cold fever

Jobs

shop assistant hairdresser teacher doctor
policewoman/policeman actress/actor vet football player

teacher
hairdresser
actress
football player
doctor
actor
vet
policeman
policewoman
shop assistant

Jobs at home

I...

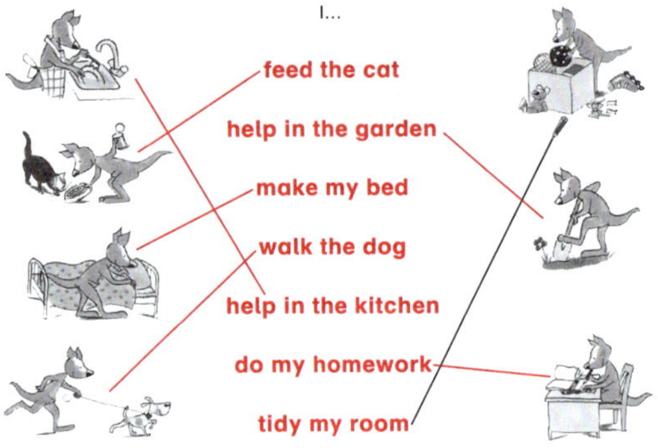

feed the cat
help in the garden
make my bed
walk the dog
help in the kitchen
do my homework
tidy my room

Germany
France
Great Britain
Spain
Poland
Turkey
Italy
USA
Russia

Italy Great Britain Turkey USA (United States of America)
Germany Russia Poland Spain France

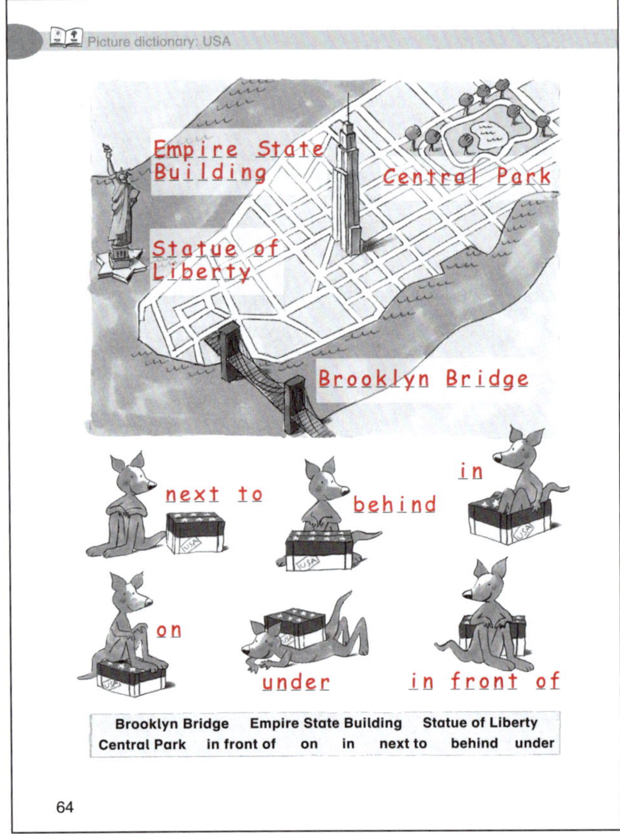

220001792

1. At the zoo you can see a lot of wild animals.
Do you know them? Write.

h _ p _ _

cr _ c _ _ i _ e

l _ o _

e _ e _ _ _ n _

gi _ a _ _ e

m _ _ k e _

k _ n _ a _ o _

z _ b _ _

elephant **lion** **giraffe** **monkey** **hippo**
zebra **crocodile** **kangaroo**

2. Match the legs to the animals. Draw lines and write.

giraffe elephant bear monkey zebra lion

3. What can the animals do? Write the correct answer.

Yes, it can. **No, it can't.**

Can a crocodile fly? ______________________

Can a hippo swim? ______________________

Can a snake jump? ______________________

Can a monkey jump? ______________________

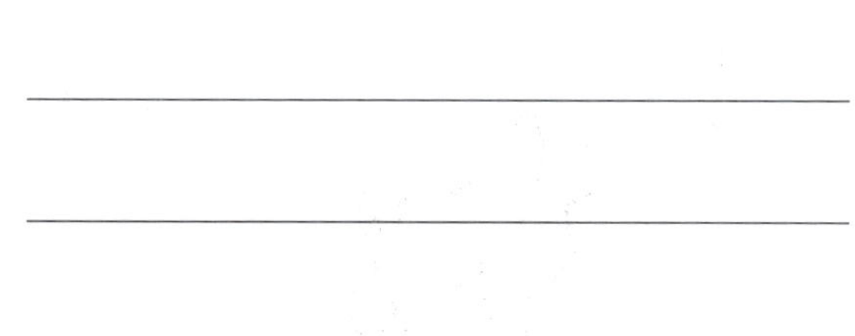

Can a bear swim? ______________________

Can a lion fly? ______________________

Richtig oder falsch?
Schreibe die Antwort auf.

4. Funny animals. Write and draw.

head: giraffe

body: lion

legs: elephant

head: ______________________

body: ______________________

legs: ______________________

head: ______________________

body: ______________________

legs: ______________________

Now draw this animal:

The head is from a kangaroo.

The body is from a hippo.

The legs are from a zebra.

5. Find out their favourite animals. Read and write.

Wir sollen die Lieblingstiere von Tim, Ben, Mary, Jenny und Sally herausfinden.

kangaroo
lion
koala
bear
snake
giraffe
hippo
elephant
zebra
crocodile
ZOO
monkey

Tim — My favourite animal is green. It has got a big mouth with sharp teeth. My favourite animal is a ______________________ .

Ben — My favourite animal is grey and has got a long nose. My favourite animal is an ______________________ .

Mary — And my favourite animal is brown and likes bananas. My ______________________ .

Jenny — My animal is brown and yellow and has got a long neck. My ______________________ .

Sally — My favourite animal is brown and can jump. My ______________________ .

6. Read the comic.

Sally and Koala at the zoo

1. Fill in.

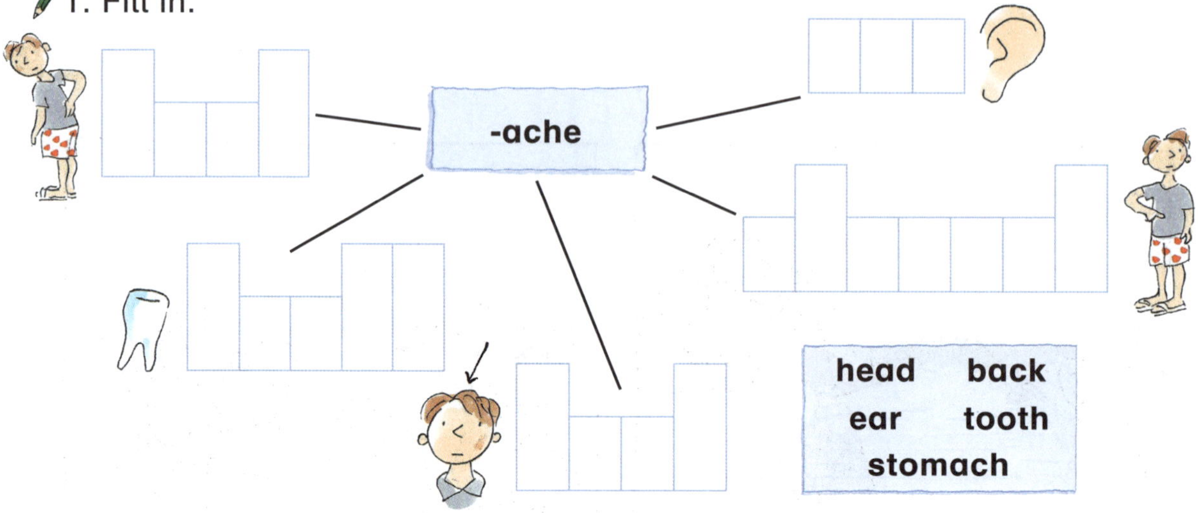

-ache

head back
ear tooth
stomach

2. Fill in and draw lines.

Sally's ear hurts. She has got an earache .

Sally's tooth hurts. She has got a ____________ .

Sally's back hurts. She has got a ____________ .

Sally's head hurts. She has got a ____________ .

Sally's stomach hurts. She has got a ____________ .

headache earache stomachache backache toothache

3. What's the matter? Read and fill in.

I have eaten 5 pizzas. — You have got a ____________________ .

I have fallen from a tree. — You have got a ____________________ .

My nose is running. — You have got a ____________________ .

My head feels hot. — You have got a ____________________ .

I have carried ten boxes of lollipops. — You have got a ____________________ .

cold	**broken arm**	**backache**	**fever**	**stomachache**

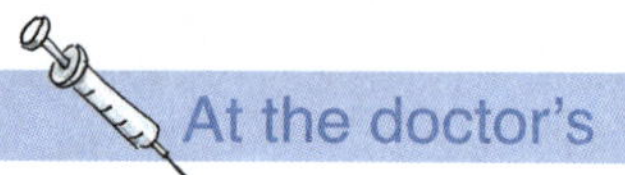

4. Read and fill in.

Ben is sitting in the ______________________ .

The ______________________ comes in and says: "Next, please!"

It's Ben's turn. The ______________________ asks Ben: "What's the matter?"

"I'm ill. I've got a ______________________ , I've got a ______________ and I think I've got a ______________ , too. I can't go to school today."

The ______________________ says: "Ben, you are not ill. Why can't you go to school today?"

"We have got a math test today, Daddy."

doctor (2x) fever nurse headache cold waiting room

5. Read the comic.

A lollipop will help

1. Guess the jobs. Write.

Sally is a ______________________ .

Sally ______________________ .

Sally ______________________ .

Sally is a ______________________ and

Koala is a ______________________ .

Sally ______________________ .

Sally is an ______________________ and

Koala is an ______________________ .

Koala is a ______________________ .

Sally is a ______________________ .

shop assistant

hairdresser

teacher

doctor

policewoman/ policeman

actress/ actor

vet

football player

2. My jobs at home. Draw lines and write.

I have to ...

make	the cat
feed	my bed
help	my room
do	in the kitchen
walk	in the garden
tidy	the dog
help	my homework

I have to make my bed.

I ____.

____.

____.

____.

____.

____.

Schaue dir die Bilder an. Was machen Sandy, Jack und Sally gerne und was nicht?

3. Look at Sandy, Jack and Sally.
Which jobs do they like and which not? Write.

SANDY

JACK

SALLY

SANDY I like to ______________________________, but
I don't like to ______________________________.

JACK I like to ______________________________, but
I don't like to ______________________________.

SALLY ______________________________,
but ______________________________.

And what about you? Write.

I ______________________________,

but ______________________________.

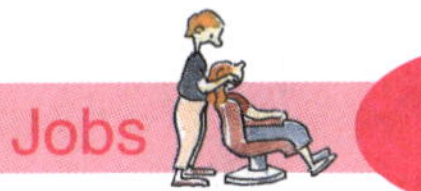

4. Read the comic.

Sally, what do you want to be?

Sally, what do you want to be?

I want to be a shop assistant.

The trousers are too small.

The shirt is too big.

No, I want to be a hairdresser.

I look horrible.

No, no, I want to be a policewoman.

Help!

TUUT!

I want to be a..., a..., a...

I just want to be a ... happy kangaroo!!!

1. Where are the children from? Write.

Turkey	Italy	USA	Russia	France	Great Britain
Spain	Germany	Poland			

 2. Guess the country. Read and write.

I love to eat baguette and croissants. I say "Bonjour!" and not "Hello!". The capital of my country is Paris.

I'm from ____________________ .

The name of our flag is Union Jack. The capital of my country is London. We have a Queen.

I'm from ____________________ .

I eat spaghetti almost every day. But I also like to eat pizza. The capital of my country is Rome.

I'm from ____________________ .

The capital of my country is Berlin. I say "Hallo!".

I'm from ____________________ .

I don't say "Hello!", I say "Merhaba!". A lot of people come to my country for their holidays.

The capital of my country is Ankara.

I'm from ____________________ .

Turkey **France** **Germany** **Italy** **Great Britain**

3. Read and fill in.

Are you from ______________________ ?

Yes, I am. Are you from ______________________ , too?

No, I'm not. I'm from ______________________ .

Are you from the ______________________ ?

No, ______________ . I'm from ______________ .

Hello, I'm from ______________________ . Are you from ______________________ , too?

No, ______________ . I'm from ______________ .

Are you from ______________________ ?

Yes, ______________ . Are you from ______________ ?

No, ______________ . I'm from ______________ .

USA Spain Poland Russia Germany Turkey Great Britain Italy

4. Read the comic.

Sally's trip around the world

1. Find the flag of the USA. Circle.

2. Do you know these New York sights? Trace the lines.

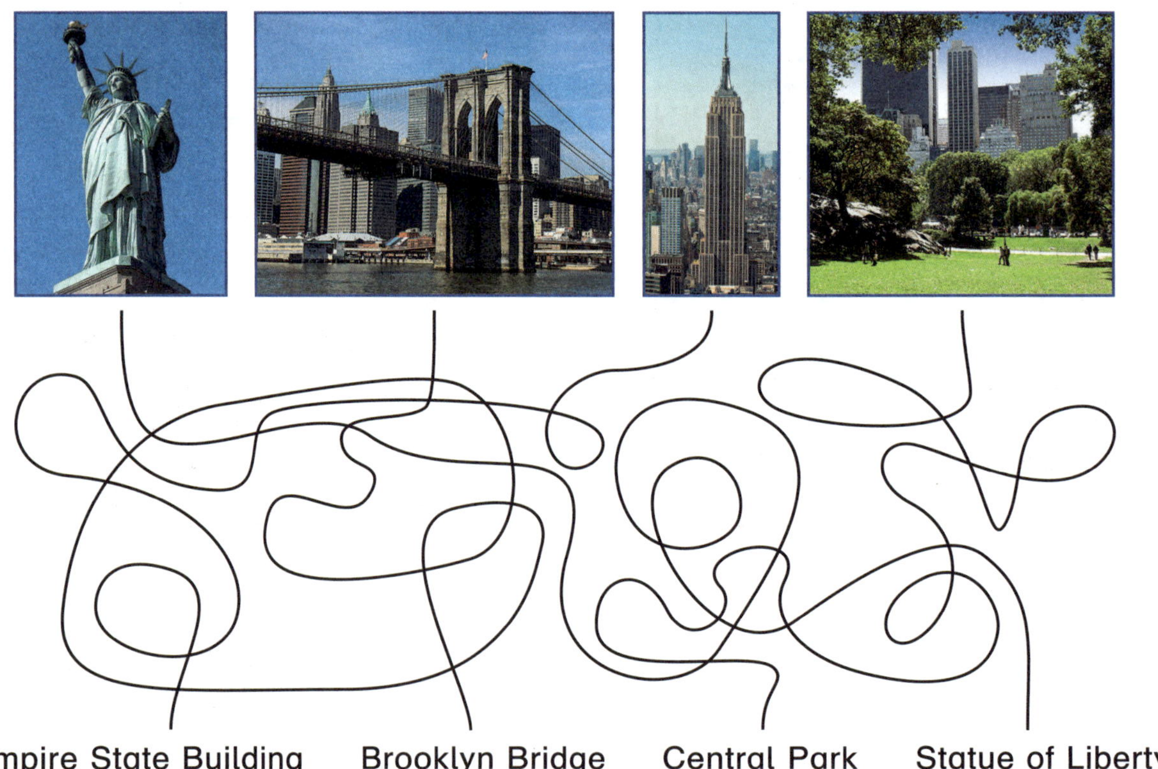

Empire State Building Brooklyn Bridge Central Park Statue of Liberty

3. Where's Sally? Draw lines and write.

Sally is...

in

in front of

behind

under

next to

on

4. Circle the correct name of the USA.

the United Stars of America

the United States of America

the United Stripes of America

5. Correct or wrong? Tick.

	correct	wrong
The name of the flag of the USA is Union Jack.	◯	◯
Americans pay with dollars and cents.	◯	◯
New York is one of the biggest cities in the USA.	◯	◯
The Empire State Building is a small house.	◯	◯
Central Park is a big park in New York.	◯	◯
The Queen is the president of the USA.	◯	◯
The people in the USA speak English.	◯	◯
The capital of the USA is London.	◯	◯
The capital of the USA is Washington D.C.	◯	◯

Du weißt schon viel über die USA.
Was stimmt und was ist falsch?
Mache einen Haken.

eleven	twelve	thirteen	fourteen	fifteen	sixteen
seventeen	eighteen	nineteen	twenty	thirty	forty
fifty	sixty	seventy	eighty	ninety	one hundred

room: __________ room: _________

room: _________

room: _________

toilet	bathroom	living room	bedroom	kitchen	
garage	garden	door	stairs	chair	table	bed
lamp	wardrobe	shelves	desk	sofa	cupboard

fish and chips
spaghetti
chicken salad
pizza
tomato

carrot soup
menu
sausage with mashed potatoes

ham
ketchup
bread
mustard
lettuce
cucumber
cheese

plate
knife
fork
spoon
to drink
to eat
sandwich

In the morning:

I get up at seven o'clock.

I have breakfast at eight o'clock.

School starts at nine o'clock.

In the afternoon:

I do my homework at three o'clock.

I play with my friends at four o'clock.

In the evening / at night:

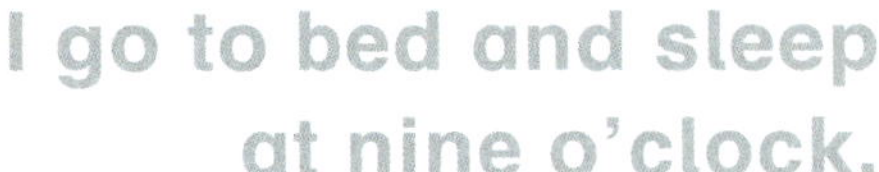

I go to bed and sleep at nine o'clock.

playing basketball

playing tennis

riding a mountain bike

riding a horse

playing football

skateboarding

reading books

swimming

inline skating

playing the piano

snowboarding

playing the guitar

ice skating

supermarket music shop clothes shop
toy shop sports shop biscuits just right
too big shoe shop too small sweet shop
spinach chocolate bars book shop

bus taxi bike car underground train lorry plane helicopter boat

straight on turn right turn left

koala zebra lion snake hippo giraffe elephant
monkey crocodile kangaroo bear

headache earache stomachache backache broken arm
toothache waiting room nurse doctor cold fever

Jobs

shop assistant	hairdresser	teacher	doctor
policewoman/policeman	actress/actor	vet	football player

Jobs at home

I...

feed the cat

help in the garden

make my bed

walk the dog

help in the kitchen

do my homework

tidy my room

_ _ _ _ _ _ _   _ _ _ _ _ _   _ _ _ _ _ _ _ _ _ _ _ _

_ _ _ _ _   _ _ _ _ _ _   _ _ _ _ _ _

_ _ _ _ _   _ _ _   _ _ _ _ _ _

Italy Great Britain Turkey USA (United States of America)
Germany Russia Poland Spain France

Brooklyn Bridge	Empire State Building	Statue of Liberty
Central Park	in front of	on	in	next to	behind	under